THE SPARE TYRE SONGBOOK

Katina Noble has always lived in London. She has known she wanted to sing and act ever since she saw Max Bygraves turn into a frog in 'The Golden Goose' in 1954. She has entertained countless children in street theatre, has performed on the top deck of a moving London bus and even played Gertrude in 'Hamlet'– outside the National Theatre! Nowadays, apart from Spare Tyre she directs and devises shows with young people and runs workshops for women with eating problems at the Women's Therapy Centre, London.

Harriet Powell grew up on a farm near Peterborough. She now lives in London with one accordian, two electric keyboards and three chaps (David, 38, Sam, 12, and Tom, 9). She recently separated from her grand piano on grounds of unreasonable size. She is a musician who has forgotten most of her classical training and a performer who learned her survival skills since 1974 in hundreds of community theatre venues, particularly over the last six wonderful years with Spare Tyre.

Clair Chapman was born in St Paul, Minnesota, USA. She was raised in the musical traditions of 'My Fair Lady' and The Weavers, with a little Gershwin on the side. She came to England in 1973 and has been in feminist theatre ever since. She is an ex-compulsive eater turned vegetarian, but she still eats her mother's herb chicken. Her song writing is based on the experience of being a compulsive eater/not being a compulsive eater, being in love/being out of love, with a little cystitis thrown in for good measure.

Judy Farrar was born in London in 1951. She has been designing and making weird and wonderful sets and props for Spare Tyre for the last six years. She has a particular passion for making life-size dummies quite a few of which, when retired from shows, tend to take up residence in her house in Hackney. She has designed for many other community and fringe theatre companies, illustrated several books, and is at present studying Art Therapy at Goldsmiths College. She has a six year old son called Stan.

Published by VIRAGO PRESS Limited 1987
41 William IV Street, London WC2N 4DB

British Library Cataloguing in Publication Data

          The Spare Tyre Songbook.
          1. Feminism – Songs and music
          2. Songs, English – Texts
          I. Spare Tyre (Theatre group)
          784.6'830542   PR119.F45

          ISBN 0-86068-858-5

Printed in Great Britain

THE
SPARE TYRE
SONGBOOK

VIRAGO

Contents

Preface
by Susie Orbach

I've always loved musicals, but in my wildest dreams I never dreamt that **Fat is a Feminist Issue** (FIFI) could ignite the imagination of a group of women actors to create words and music for not simply one, but a handful of poignant, funny and inspirational plays about women's relationship to food and body image. I mean it's hardly showbiz material – women alternatively starving themselves, scavenging food, hanging over toilet bowls vomiting up huge quantities of speedily ingested food. In fact, when I first recieved a letter from Clair Chapman asking if she could see me with a view to writing a play based on FIFI, I was perplexed. What on earth could she mean? A worthy documentary perhaps – an attack on the food and fashion industries, the role of food in the family and women's special relationship to it? But a play with music, surely not?

A few weeks later we met over lunch. I was in two minds. Part of me was bemused and intrigued, excited at the idea that FIFI could be dramatised, but part of me thought the idea was nuts. I just couldn't fathom how you could make a sympathetic entertainment out of women's agonising relationship to food, fat and thin.

Six months later, I sat sobbing my eyes out, jaws aching from laughter, exhilarated by Spare Tyre's first play **Baring the Weight**. Thinking of it now, I recall the feeling of lightness and freedom that I and the rest of the audience felt in seeing our experience accurately understood and compassionately expressed. I couldn't believe what they had achieved. It was so wonderful.

When I was writing **Fat is a Feminist Issue II** in 1981, I knew that I would be dedicating it to Spare Tyre. For FIFI II was a tribute to their work and in part a consequence of it. In the first book I had sketched a model for self-help groups to help women begin to look at their compulsive eating (or food avoidance), in order to find a way to intervene in what is so often a very painful and obsessive relationship with food. I had proposed a self-help model on pragmatic and political grounds. At The Women's Therapy Centre, there simply weren't enough workers experienced in this approach to eating problems to provide ongoing therapy groups for all the women who wanted them. My own experience in working through this problem had been in a self-help group, called together in New York City at the height of the Women's Liberation Movement in 1970. The group had affected me profoundly, not only helping me with my own eating problem but politicising an area that had before felt more like straightforward personal failure. In beginning to work as a psychotherapist with women who had similar problems, I felt the group approach could be very helpful.

Spare Tyre not only made us laugh and weep over our eating problems, they also encouraged women to try and do something different about them. They took up the message of self-help and spread it everywhere, joyfully and seriously. In mother-and-toddler groups, on the feminist theatre circuit, in diet clubs, they took their plays and skits and their enthusiasm for the anti-diet method around the UK and Europe. But they did more than this. They set up scores of groups on their travels – groups that helped hundreds of individual women who had been isolated in their own distress to find new respect for themselves, and the courage to face the complex of issues in their lives that came to be expressed in compulsive eating. It was because of the number of groups that Spare Tyre and The Women's Therapy Centre generated, and the questions that those groups came up with, that I found I needed to extend the ideas of Fat is a Feminist Issue into a more explicit guide to self-help.

I love their plays, I love their songs, I love their energy. My only complaint, voiced yearly and borne with polite tolerance by the Spare Tyres, is that I desperately want a walk-on part and they just won't give me one!

Susie Orbach
London
August 1986

Acknowledgements

Production

Judy Farrar	Design and cartoons
Harriet Powell	Arrangements
John Barker	Music settings
Martin Haswell	Photographs

Additional Photographs: Alexia Cross, Sarah Ainslie, Lesley MacIntyre, Anita Corbyn

Thanks also to:

The Original Spare Tyre

Sylvia Hallett, Nancy Roberts, Shane Vahey, Janine Turkie, Adele Saleem, Caroline Eves, Joanne Richler, Tina McHugh, Tish Francis, Val Warburton

Our Trustees

Peter and Patricia Diggory, Judy Cook, Tony Vaughn, Lennie Goodings, Susie Orbach, Carry Gorney, Anna Wing

Our 'Team'

Claire Grove, Debbie Shewell, Tasha Fairbanks	Direction
Judy Farrar	Design
Janice May, Pat Lacey, Katrina Duncan	Administration and finance
Beth Hardisty, Ronnie Wood, Marilyn Eccles	Lights

Guiding Lights and Moral Support

Susie Orbach, David, Sam and Tom Powell, Rene Rice, Geraldine Caldwell, Pete Mount, Ian Litterick, Tom Stevens, Women's Therapy Centre, Pookie Hareduke, Kathryn Johnson, Alasdair Cameron, The Rubber Jennies, Monica Strauss, Inter-Action, Oval Printshop, Peter and Mary Noble, Kara, Martha Powell, Clair's Family, all the funding bodies who have supported us, especially the GLC, and all our audiences from Belfast to Brighton and everywhere in between

People we've Stayed with on Tour

Jane and David (Manchester), Jackie and Alan (Leeds), Jenny (Sheffield), Lucy (Portsmouth), Janice and Alan (Bristol), Carol (Southampton), Maria (Belfast), Caroline (Liverpool), Dick and Kate (Newcastle), Vivien (Glasgow), Clare (Edinburgh), Susie (Frome), Pete and Debbie (Bristol), David and Jennifer (Peterborough), Sandie (Norwich), Pam and David (Edinburgh), Sheryl (Lancaster) and all the 'one night stands' too numerous to mention

Spare Tyre sells three cassette tapes of their songs – all the songs in this book and more!

> Eat It - If You Want To!
> Second Helpings
> Laugh Lines

are available from: Spare Tyre Tapes
86 Holmleigh Road
London N16 5PY
Tel: 01-800 9099

Introduction
by Spare Tyre

In 1978 a revolutionary new book was published, **Fat is a Feminist Issue**, by Susie Orbach. Its message: diets don't work, women eat out of emotional more than physical hunger, and ninety-five percent of all women who diet put some or all of the weight back on. It had a spectacular impact on millions of women who had been tormenting themselves on diets for years.

In 1979 Clair Chapman put an ad in Time Out: 'Women interested in putting together a play based on **Fat is a Feminist Issue** write to Clair.' The response was incredible. Women of all ages, shapes and theatrical experience wrote in, auditions were held, and out of these Spare Tyre was born.

We began as a group committed to taking the anti-diet message to a wider audience. Our first three shows were full of sketches about cream cakes and plastic track suits, and our songs about the agonies of life as a compulsive eater:

> I'm putting it off 'til I'm thinner
> All of this just isn't me
> I'll stop being a mess and become a success
> But I'm putting it off – 'til I'm seven stone three.

We always wrote songs out of our own experience. All of us had been that woman sitting in her room, feeling fat, unable to do anything with her life until she'd slimmed down to the magic weight.

We've moved on to other subjects and we've kept that personal link. We write songs about our lives – about children, loneliness, parents, men, guilt. We also write songs in response to political events – the Wendy Savage case, life under Mrs T., Victoria Gillick's campaign. And sure enough, women in our audiences respond with tears of laughter and recognition.

Seven years, seven productions and hundreds of performances later, we're still together, travelling the length and breadth of the country with our pianos, giant puppets, props and ladders. We assemble our sets, play our own music, write our own songs and sketches. Our format is simple: comic cabaret sprinkled with songs – humour and music have been the cornerstone of our work.

These songs are pieces of our lives. We hope you enjoy them.

Eating Your Heart Out

I'm gon-na be eight stone by my birth-day In hot pants by Ju-ly —— I'll start my fast to- mor-row— but to-day — I'll bake a pie ——.

Pounds

by Clair Chapman

If you've got a bit to lose, come to me, I've been fat and so I know it's not ea-sy. Give your mon-ey to me and you'll be fine, There's a meet-ing ev-'ry week at two pounds a time.

CHORUS

Pounds! I want to take them off you, I have a meth-od that a-stounds.

last time to Coda

Pounds! I want to rake them off you, Pounds and pounds and pounds.

CODA

Pounds and pounds and pounds and pounds and pounds and pounds!

If you've got a bit to lose, come to me
I've been fat and so I know it's not easy
Give your money to me and you'll be fine
There's a meeting every week — at two pounds a time

    CHORUS
    Pounds! I want to take them off you
    I have a method that astounds
    Pounds! I want to rake them off you
    Pounds and pounds and pounds

We will help you fight the flab, that's our job
But you'll have to keep it off, you great slob
It's a piece of cake (ha ha ha!) to get down to goal
But you'll almost all regain it – you've no self-control

    CHORUS

This year we've grossed one hundred million pounds flat
This dieting business is getting rather fat!
Give us your money, we'll slim you, goodbye and good luck my dear
We'll see you back at square one – at this time next year

    CHORUS
    Pounds! I want to take them off you
    I have a method that astounds
    Pounds! I want to rake them off you
    Pounds and pounds and pounds and pounds and pounds . . .
                              and pounds!

Mars Bar

by Clair Chapman

Why is it
Every time my mother rings me on the phone
I want a Mars Bar?
Is this the thing that
Pavlov did with those dogs?

What is it
About my mother's 'Hello sweetheart!' makes me scream
I need a Mars Bar?
Mummy and chocolate
Melted up there in the cogs

She lives in misery
Every day of her life
'Please God!' she prays, 'My Joanne
Make her somebody's wife . . .'
                    (Oy vai, Mom!)

Here I am
My mother rings me on the phone
And here I am
And here's my Mars Bar!
Well, cheers, Mom – you've made me what I am today
And cheers to the Scarsdale diet – hip hip . . . hooray. . .

I'm Putting It Off 'til I'm Thinner

by Clair Chapman

I'd like to go out to parties
Fancy dress and crazy hat
But if I went out
I know they'd all shout
'Look at her! Isn't she fat!' – so

CHORUS
I'm putting it off 'til I'm thinner
All of this just isn't me
I'll stop being a mess and become a success
But I'm putting it off – 'til I'm seven stone
three

I'd really like to go swimming
Play tennis or some other sport
But I'd take off my jacket
And pick up a racket
And I know I'd get laughed off the court – so

CHORUS

Things will be fine when I'm thinner
All of my worries will stop
I'll have a job and a lover
Finally I'll be on top – well, maybe

I'd like to turn heads as I step out
Even the pigeons would pause
I'd sail down the street
They'd fall at my feet
'Til then – I'm staying indoors – 'cos

CHORUS

Who'd give a job to a fat girl
Clearly so out of control
One day I'll go for that perfect job
One day I'll get off the dole – well, maybe

I'd like to go out in the big world
Be bright and sparkling and gay
Drive fast cars at night
And eat Turkish Delight
And not give a damn what I weigh – but

CHORUS

Inside Every Fat Person

by Clair Chapman

Intro: (Joanne has stopped dieting. Daphne is The Slimmer of the Year)

Jo: Inside every fat person there's a thin one trying to escape
         I used to diet and diet to let the skinny one out
         I thought the Hattie Jacques that looked like me
         Concealed a tiny Vivien Leigh –
         I've just found out that's not what it's all about

Daph: I thought he'd love the thin one inside all of that flesh
         I knew that he'd adore me, I hadn't any doubt,
         A skinny little beauty who'd lost six stone
         Could call her husband her very own –
         I've just found out that's not what it's all about

Jo: It's me
Daph: He wouldn't love me if I weighed eight stone
Jo: All me
Daph: I just can't win
Jo: It's mine
Daph: He wouldn't love me if I looked like Jane Fonda
Jo: All mine
Daph: What's the point of being thin?
Jo: Every bit of it is mine
Daph: What's the point of being thin?
Jo: Every bit of it is mine
Daph: What's the point of being thin?

Jo: And now I've discovered it's all the same me
         At eight stone seven or fourteen three
         I've just found out
         That that's what it's all about

Before ....   After.....

Choc 'n' Roll

by Katina Noble

Give me fresh pas-ta swim-ming in cream, Las-ag-ne, mac-a-ron-i, oh - oh ___ I could scream, Smoth-er them in but-ter, grease drip-ping down your chin, Gar-lic bread and pan-cakes, so who wants to be thin? I'm a

CHORUS

real big eat-er ___ I got a huge ap-pe-tite ___ I'm a great big eat-er, You won't push me out of sight. Screw 'em all (screw 'em all!) Gim-me more of that pie (more of that pie!) And here's what I got to say: ___ I'm a real big eat-er ___ I got a huge ap-pe-tite ___ I'm a great big eat-er, You won't push me out of sight. ___

Give me fresh pasta swimming in cream
Lasagne, macaroni, oh-oh I could scream
Smother them in butter, grease dripping down your chin
Garlic bread and pancakes, so who wants to be thin?

> CHORUS
> I'm a real big eater
> I got a huge appetite
> I'm a great big eater
> You won't push me out of sight

I want chocolate mousse, lemon meringue pie
Blackcurrant fool to blow me sky high
Cheesecake with chocolate – my oh my
I'm gonna sit right down and eat them up, don't ask me why

> CHORUS

I want Aeros, Yorkies, a million chocolate bars
Smarties, Flakes, Maltesers and Mars
I want all the chocolate I could ever consume
I'm gonna move myself a sweetshop right into my room

> CHORUS

They say, 'Tut, tut! Oo! Should you be eating that?
You've gotta watch your figure or you're gonna get fat!'
The next man who does that, I'm gonna put him in his place
I'm gonna take my bowl of chocolate mousse and shove it in his face!

> CHORUS

Everyone says you mustn't, it's naughty not nice,
Don't indulge, don't enjoy or you will pay the price.
They deny us pleasures in every single way
Well, screw 'em all (screw 'em all!)
Gimme more of that pie (more of that pie!)
And here's what I got to say:

> CHORUS

How Do I Look?

Dye it

Cut it

Grow it

Pluck it

Loose it

Hide it

Instant Allure

Cover Up

Smell Gone

You'd really be quite attractive if only you'd smile a bit more....

Mmmm – Nice – Shame about the face
She'd look all right if she lost a couple of stone
Cor . . . Couldn't get many of them in a bucket
Mmmm – Nice – Shame about the body
Should you be eating that?
Wouldn't kick her out of bed

He Touched Me There

by Clair Chapman

Such A Pretty Face

by Clair Chapman

Gently-with a rocking bass

Pic-ture all the love-ly girls at Cind-y's wed-ding show-er. They give her pret-ty pres-ents and in-dulge in mer-ry chat. They all wish her the best of things, A hap-py life, con-tent-ed home.

Sand-ie wish-es Cind-y would get fat.

CHORUS

That's the old-er one stand-ing in the corn-er, Stuff-ing in the choc-'late cake, dread-ful dis-grace.

Cind-y's the pret-ty one, Sand-ie's the fat one,

It's such a pit-y, she's got such a pret-ty face.

face.

Slower

face. It's such a pit-y, she had such a pret-ty face.

Picture all the lovely girls at Cindy's wedding shower
They give her pretty presents and indulge in merry chat
They all wish her the best of things
A happy life, contented home –
Sandie wishes Cindy would get fat

    CHORUS
    That's the older one standing in the corner
    Stuffing in the chocolate cake, dreadful disgrace
    Cindy's the pretty one, Sandie's the fat one
    It's such a pity, she's got such a pretty face

Picture pretty Cindy looking like a walking wedding dream
Size ten satin with flowers in her hair
Everything is beautiful
Just one thing to spoil it –
The size eighteen pink whale over there

    CHORUS
    That's the older one standing in the corner
    Stuffing in the wedding cake, dreadful disgrace
    Cindy's the pretty one, Sandie's the fat one
    It's such a pity, she's got such a pretty face

Christmas time in forty years, everyone's at Cindy's
All her kids and grandkids are around her everywhere
Warmness and happiness
Everyone loves everyone
Except Aunt Sandie over there

    CHORUS
    That's the older one standing in the corner
    Stuffing in the Christmas cake, dreadful disgrace
    Cindy's the pretty one, Sandie's the fat one
    It's such a pity, she had such a pretty face

    It's such a pity, she had such a pretty face

Body Perm

by Harriet Powell

We performed this spoken over a slow swing beat

Harriet:
Well, I'm feeling so low as I walk by the hairdresser's shop
I think a quick wash and a blow-dry might help cheer me up, so I stop
Or maybe some streaks or highlights, that'll help brighten up my life
But I should have known better, 'cos Zak knows better than me

Hairdresser:
Now what you really need for hair so lank and thin
Is more than a wash, and more than a trim
Take a look at this picture and see what you think to
A body perm!

Harriet:
Now if I could look like that! But I'm half-filled with horror and dread
A perm means curls and my body would rather be dead
Than be a Shirley Temple look a like, I'd rather just be me
I should have known better – but Zak persuaded me

Hairdresser:
Now it won't be curly and it won't be frizzy
It's just the style if your lifestyle's busy
You know I'm right, it's only eighteen quid, have
A body perm!

Harriet:
Now as the curlers go in, I'm filled with doubt and anxiety
I want to say stop, then he offers me a coffee or tea
I try to relax, everything will be just fine
I know it's only hair – but, Zak, that hair is mine!

Hairdresser:
We're nearly done, we'll just take off the neutraliser
Not feeling nervous, are we? Your friends won't recognize you
Oh, it's come out nice! Now aren't you glad you had
A body perm?

Harriet:
(HORRIFIED GASP)
Well I look into the mirror and the tears well in my eyes
There's a lump in my throat, and I try to hide my sobs and sighs
('It's very nice!')
It's not what he promised, but I just can't make a fuss
(I can't go out like this!)
I know it doesn't matter, but it makes me look much fatter
I know I shouldn't care, it's only my hair
If it's confidence I lack, it won't come from Zak, but Zak –
I want my lank, thin, straight hair
BACK!!!

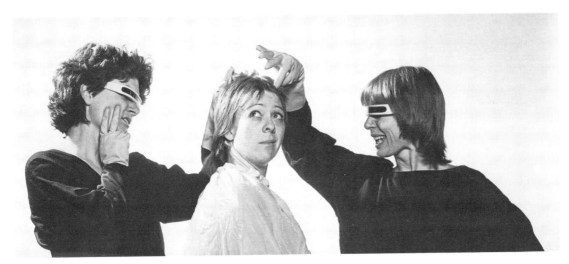

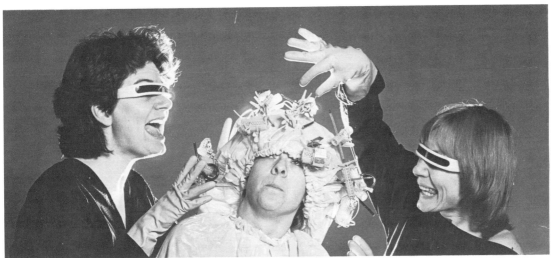

Suntan Blues

by Clair Chapman

I've got those skin as white as driven snow
Sunbeds make my freckles show blues

I've got those sat out in the yard all week
Still look like a paleface freak blues

I've got a big, pink glowing nose
(Is that why they call me an English Rose?)

I've got those skin as white as driven snow
Sunbeds make my freckles show blues

I've got those maybe Burgasol's the answer
Never mind it gives you cancer blues

I've got those everyone says I look sick
Gotta get a tan real quick blues

I look so white and pale
That I feel like the great white whale

I've got those maybe Burnasun's the answer
Never mind it gives you cancer blues

I've got those fried my skin in Tenerife
Tried to fry my skin in Greece blues

I've got those peeled off until it was gone
Creamed and stuck the peels back on blues

I go out to have a good time
They're all looking at my bathing suit line

I've got those fried my skin in Tenerife
Tried to fry my skin in Greece blues

I've got those haven't I had lots of fun
Sitting in the summer sun blues

I've got those blisters, blotches, carcinosis
Sunstroke and a tan neurosis blues

Wish I lived in a bygone age
When a snowwhite skin was all the rage
I've got those haven't I had lots of fun
(and so I'm sure has everyone)
lying in oblivion
frying 'til you're overdone, oh
haven't I had lots of fun
lying in the summer sun blues?

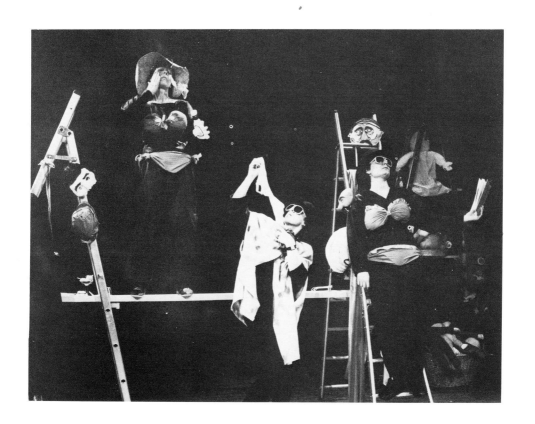

Gotta Love It

by Clair Chapman

Love it love it, gotta love it
Love my flabby thighs and bum
Really love my every wrinkle
And adore my sagging tum

Eat it eat it, do I want to eat it?
Am I hungry, am I bored, frustrated, angry?
Love it love it, gotta love it
All of it is me

Everyone around me from my mother to the magazines
Tells me I'm not up to scratch, ties me in a knot
I should search inside myself and teach myself to love myself
Learn to accept what I've got. Yuk!

Love it love it, gotta love it
Love the parts I hate the worst
Really love all my obessions
Hang myself, but love them first

Eat it eat it, do I want to eat it
Am I hungry, am I bored, frustrated, angry?
Love it love it, gotta love it
All of it is me

Everyone around me from my lover to the media
Tells me I'm not good enough – what is this, a plot?
I should look at all of me and see that I'm all right as me
Stop trying to be what I'm not – oh . . .

Love it love it, gotta love it, all of it is me
Love it love it, gotta love it, all of it is me
Love it love it, gotta love it, all of it is me

How Do I Look?

by Clair Chapman

If the earth flooded and the trees fell down
And the Post Office Tower burnt to the ground
We'd still be saying 'How do I look?'
But that's the way they like us, honey
They're just happy making money
Selling insecurities by hook and by crook

CHORUS
Wish I could rise above it
Wish I could tell them,'Shove it!'
How can I learn to love it?
How do I look?

Models smirking everywhere
Perfect bodies, teeth, eyes, hair
And we keep saying 'How do I look?'
What do I want the world to say
It's nothing to do with what I weigh
I want something back — that somebody took

CHORUS

If Margaret Thatcher fell from power (HURRAY
And I stepped in at the eleventh hour
They'd all be saying 'How does she look?'
Another lady boss, that's great –
Who's her fella? What's her weight?
What's her favourite flower?
Favourite perfume? Can she cook?

I'm going to rise above it
I'm going to tell them, 'Shove it!'
'Cos I already love it
Here's how I look!

Doesn't it Make You Sick?

Well actually I was waiting for a pregnancy test...

Sorry to keep you waiting, Madam, but Doctor's terribly busy today...

The coil has been tested on a number of women with only two deaths and a small amount of infertility...

Pop your feet into the stirrups, Madam, and relax your knees...

We don't know what you have. It's non-specific...

Any pain, vomiting, abnormal bleeding – just give us a ring...

MADAM, pop your feet into the stirrups and relax your knees — ...

RELAX YOUR KNEES

Just Take This And Give It To The Chemist

by Clair Chapman

Patient: Oh, hello, Doctor —

Doctor: You have three minutes. Problem?

Patient: Well it's like this. I haven't been sleeping very well lately –

Doctor: Just take this and give it to the chemist
(SINGS) Pay the price and you're home free
Just take this and give it to the chemist
When you imbibe
What I prescribe
There's a little bribe for me

Patient: Doctor, Doctor, I need someone to talk to
With husband, kids and work I'm really getting in a mess
I don't want pills or potions or prescriptions
I need someone to lean on, to cope with the stress

Doctor: Just take this and give it to the chemist
I have no time to talk it through
Just take this and give it to the chemist
We've just begun
We're overrun
And everyone's like you

Patient: Doctor, Doctor, you've got to help me
My son's got yellow fever and my mother's sniffing glue
My auntie's got rabies, I fear that I might catch it
My old man is a junkie . . . Doctor, tell me what to do

Doctor: Just take this and give it to the chemist
I know best so don't you worry
Just take this and give it to the chemist
Your time is up
Your time is up
Your time is up – NEXT PLEASE!

If I were you I'd spend a couple of weeks in bed . . . .

The Smoking Song

by Harriet Powell

(<u>Sing to well known tune!</u>)

Smoking a cigarette again, never wanted to, what am I to do?
I can't help it. . .

I had my first cigarette on the bus home from school
I looked so cool – what a fool!
My mother saw my guilty face, couldn't hide the smell away
As I did the empty packs — ten Woodbine a day

    CHORUS
    A moment on the lips is a lifetime in their grip
    And you and I will die from my cigarettes, cigarettes
    Smoke gets in your eyes, up your nose, in your hair
    In your clothes, everywhere is smoke

And then in London, a student, alone in my flat
With a neurotic cat, getting fat
No money, no friends, smoking mealtimes away
A great way to diet — twenty roll-ups a day

    CHORUS

When I was pregnant I was happy, with a wonderful bloke
We both gave up the smoke – what a joke!
The baby arrived, someone said 'Celebrate!'
So I had a puff (he didn't), now it's thirty B & H

    CHORUS

Now when I light up a cigarette and my kids ask me why
I want to die, and I cry
When they recoil from my kisses, but there's worse to come yet –
I dreamt my son was smoking, just one cigarette

Yippee! Pregnancy!

by Harriet Powell

Yippee! Pregnancy!
This is going to be fun
I'll be healthy and glowing, I'll do everything
right
(Iron pills, no smoking, bed early every night)
No need to care what size my belly or arse is
And if anybody asks 'Are you going to the classes?'
Of course! Whatever's best for baby and me
Oh, yes – naturally!

The relaxation classes make you feel just great
But at the antenatal clinic you just wait
(And wait. . . and wait. . .)
Waiting to be seen, hour after hour
Like rows of cows in a milking parlour
Giving urine samples, pint after pint
You wait in a cubicle in solitary confinement
You wonder, have they forgotten me?
Of course they have — naturally

Yippee! Pregnancy!
They tell you at the classes what to do
How to breathe and relax with each
contraction
'Our easy method will see you through the
action!
Pethidine or epidural you won't need
I hope, by the way, you plan to breastfeed.'
Of course! Whatever's best for baby and me
Oh, yes – naturally!

When you're overdue, not feeling so great
Still waiting at the clinic and you're feeling the
weight
(The weight . . . the weight . . .)
Waiting around, what's the use
Then they book you in for Friday, nine o'clock
to induce

Well, you feel such a failure, you know it's not
right –
They told you at the classes – so you try to fight
But the doctors say they know what's best for
me
For them, they mean — naturally

Yippee, Pregnancy!
Well, that was fun
Now on the day I become someone's mum
First it's an enema up the bum
Then a shave (this isn't what the classes
taught us!)
And it's on to the bed to break the waters
The contractions start – clever me!
At least I'm still breathing — naturally!

Several attempts to get the drip in the vein
Thank God I learned to cope with the pain
(The pain . . . the pain . . .)
Painful contractions, while they assess
Whether the baby is in distress
It's not, but I am — I think I'm gonna crack
With all this pressure on my back
Can't I have a bit of help from gravity
Is that too much to ask? – naturally

Yippee! – Pregnancy –
We're almost done
Now you're having epidural or pethidine
(I don't want either, but I give in)
Induction, pethadine, episiotomy
Pull it out, stitch me up, and have your cup of
tea
Pity, with all your technology
Babies can't slip out — naturally!

SPOKEN: And who's left holding the baby? ME!

Cystitis

by Clair Chapman

I got that old familiar feeling. . . cystitis

    In the morning I wake up. Will I pay for that roll in the hay
    Last night? I stumble to the toilet to start my day
    My eyes are bleary, my head's unclear
    I sit there waiting and what do I hear?

I hear nothing . . . nothing . . . nothing . . . nothing . . .
I got that old familiar feeling . . . if you know what I mean

    Well, I down a pint of water, a pot of marshmallow tea
    I'll just quickly go to the toilet to have myself a pee
    I'm sure I'm really all right, it was just a mistake
    But my eyes start to water and I feel that old, familiar ache

And I get nothing . . . nothing . . . nothing . . . nothing . . .

    I start drinking lemon barley, put away that Nescafé
    I'll just go to the loo (I had so much to do today!)

I got that old familiar feeling – and it's driving me to drink
(and drink . . . and drink . . . and drink!)

    By midday I'm in floods of tears and totally obsessed
    Pacing from the bathroom to the bedroom, haven't even got dressed
    Clutching my hot water bottle and my Woman's Own
    I decide to ring the doctor and I stagger to the phone

Trying to get something . . . anything . . . SOMETHING . . . ANYTHING!

    He gives me antibiotics (so what's new?) and I begin
    By next week I will have thrush, I just can't win

I got that old familiar feeling . . . that I just can't win

    Well, they've found a cure for smallpox, a vaccine for polio
    Jabs for typhoid, yellow fever, so the nasties will not grow
    But when it comes to women's waterworks all you get is pills and chat
    If men got cystitis, you'd get a helluva lot more than that

But men? Get nothing . . . nothing . . . nothing . . . nothing . . .

I got that old familiar feeling . . . I can't wee and I can't win

Hank Wangford

by Clair Chapman

Well, I went down to the family planning clinic the other day
I'd had it with the pill and I had thrown my cap away
My boyfriend took the Durex and slung 'em out of bed
So I reckoned it was time to give the coil a chance instead
(Lippes Loop, Multi load, Copper Seven and Copper T!)

I rolled up to the clinic, they told me to sit down
So I picked up a magazine and started to look around
The nurse called me and undressed me, and I started to sweat
And then came the moment I shall never forget

    CHORUS
    Hank Wangford was gonna to put my coil in!
    Hank Wangford was gonna to put my coil in!
    I thought I was prepared for whatever was to come
    I'd even taken Valium
    But I wasn't prepared for Hank Wangford putting my coil in!

I said, 'Now, hey there, Mister, did I not see you last night?'
He looked extremely pleased, and then he said, 'You got it right
On Wednesday nights we play at the Old Bull and Bumble Bee –'
'This may be true,' said I to him, 'but you won't play with me!'

(Keep your cotton pickin' fingers where they belong on them guitar strings!)

At first he smiled and tears of laughter then came streaming down
But he sobered up when he saw that I would not be brought around
He stood swiftly to attention: 'Madam, you have gone too far!'
I says, 'Would you let Mick Jagger change the engine on your car?'

    CHORUS

And then a little voice inside me said:
'If Hank Wangford's not gonna to put your coil in, what will you do then?
If you say no to birth control, you'll have to give up men . . .'
That's not a bad idea, says I, but hang on, listen here
I been gittin' a few ideas from a gal called Germaine Greer
(Coitus interruptus is the only way to fly!)

Weeks later my boyfriend's a nervous wreck and my sheets are in a mess
And withdrawal hasn't done me a lot of good, I must confess
So before we split up entirely, there's one thing left to try
Forgiveness is divine, please, doctor, listen to my cry

    Dr Wangford, please put my coil in!
    Dr Wangford, please put my coil in!
    If it hurts I will keep mum, hell, I'll o.d. on valium
    Dr Wangford please put – Dr Wangford please put –
    Hank Wangford, won't you please put my coil in!

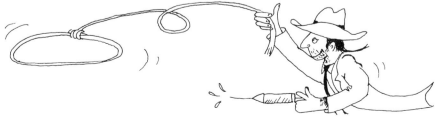

Temptations

by Harriet Powell

(ii) Lead us in-to the paths of self-right-eous-ness _____ *(all)* And de - liv-er us from the ev - ils of

Ang - er, de-press-ion, frus - tra - tion _____ And from temp-ta-tion in the wil _____ der -

ness, A _____ men. *(picks up fags)* *(i)* Kids!

(picks up KitKat) *(picks up drink)* unaccompanied *(over 'Casio' slow swing beat)*

(ii) Why did-n't he ring? *(iii)* Who cares? *(i)* I wake up in the morn-ing and

light my first cig-a-rette, May-be it will help to get the morn-ing _____ un-der-way. I

could-n't do _____ a thing with - out that first cig-a-rette, I need my lit - tle pleas-ures to

get me through the day. *(ii)* I could-n't do with-out my Kit Kat with each cof-fee,

Cup of cof-fee, Kit Kat and an - oth - er fag. I could-n't do with-out those

lit-tle things to get me through The day would be a real _____ drag. *(iii)* At

lunch I have a glass of wine _____ And by the fourth or fifth I'm feel-ing fine, _____ With

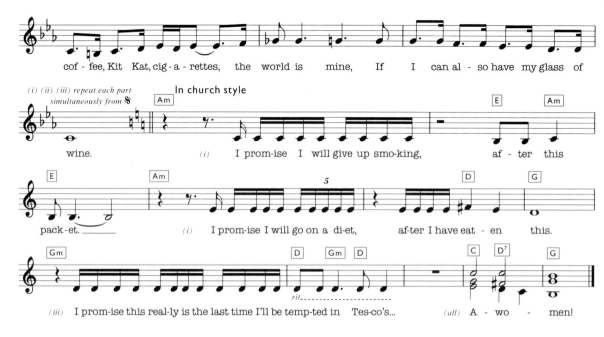

cof - fee, Kit Kat, cig - a - rettes, the world is mine, If I can al - so have my glass of

(i) (ii) (iii) repeat each part simultaneously from 𝄋

In church style

Am   E   Am

wine.   (i)   I prom - ise I will give up smo - king,   af - ter this

E   Am   5   D   G

pack - et. _____   (i)   I prom - ise I will go on a di - et,   af - ter I have eat - en   this.

Gm   D   Gm D   C   D⁷   G

(iii) I prom - ise this real - ly is the last time I'll be temp - ted in   Tes - co's...   (all) A - wo - men!

rit _____

46

Mother's Courage

Take the goldfish out of your pocket, darling . . . No, it doesn't want to play with you. It's going to die if you don't put it back in the water . . . Yes, it does look very sweet in your pencil case, but it's going to die if you don't put it back in the water. TAKE IT OUT of your mouth, it is going to DIE if you DON'T PUT IT BACK IN THE WATER!

You've Gotta Be Kidding!

by Clair Chapman

When you're into your twenties and you haven't had a baby yet
You might be pleased, and you might be upset
You might be full of anxious compunction
'Cos your body hasn't fulfilled its natural function

Natural function ... natural function

    Biology
    Starts to desecrate the body that stayed up til three
    Easily (once upon a time).
    Statistics
    About the Elderly Primigravida
    Seem pessimistic
    Suddenly

On the one hand you might be overjoyed
At what you've managed to avoid
There's wine, not Ribena in your refrigerator
Who needs a baby when you've got an alligator?

Alligator ... alligator

On the other hand you might be quite excited
You've got a baby and you're delighted
And if sleepless nights make you feel a bit glum
You can give it a cuddle and bite it on the bum

On the bum ... on the bum

    Biology
    Starts to indicate it's time to see if babies
    Are for me.
    Twinges
    When I see chubby little cherubs
    Lead to binges
    Frequently

And now everything starts to feel a bit strange
You could be changing nappies while you go through the change
You could decide to give the whole business a miss
But doesn't it make you a woman, this?
Make you a woman (it's about time)
Make you a woman (it's about time)

You're in your thirties now and you look at the others
All your friends are becoming mothers
You look around, you open your eyes
It's now or never and you realise–

You've gotta be kidding! What about my career?
You've gotta be kidding! I hope I don't do it wrong
You've gotta be kidding! Will it make me feel sick?
You've gotta be kidding! Will I be up all night long?
You've gotta be kidding! Change is as good as a rest
You've gotta be kidding! What if it falls out of its cot?
You've gotta be kidding! What if it's what I think I really want now
                But I have it, and it's not ...?
          You've gotta be kidding!

Dishpan Hands

by Clair Chapman

Slow 50s rock

My mum said that mar-riage was where it was all at, A life for two, (him and you) in a cos-y lit-tle flat. I pict-ured my-self ent-er - tain-ing, cook-ing Cord-on Bleu souff - lés, But now I've got my - self stuck in, I'm see-ing through the haze, 'cos I've got Dish - pan hands,

Ooh aah ooh house-maid's

Ooh aah ooh *Ooh aah ooh*

Oohaah ooh *Oohaah ooh* *Oohaah ooh* *Ooh aah ooh* *Oohaah ooh*

knee, Hoo - ver el-bow, that's what mar - riage means to me. My

Ooh *aah* *ooh* *aah*

cul - in - a - ry cre - a - tions are cour-te-sy of Peek Freans,

last time to Coda

2nd time D.%. al Coda

Walls pork pies, Bird's Eye peas, Cord - on Bleu baked beans.

⊕ **CODA** Slower

(all) Walls pork pies, aah *Bird's Eye peas, aah* *Cord - on Bleu baked beans.*
Walls pork pies, Bird's Eye peas, Cord - on Bleu baked beans.

rit

* *(backing voices in smaller notes)*

My mum said that marriage was where it was all at
A life for two (him and you) in a cosy little flat
I pictured myself entertaining, cooking Cordon Bleu soufflés
But now I've got myself stuck in, I'm seeing through the haze – 'cos I've got

Dishpan hands, housemaid's knee
Hoover elbow, that's what marriage means to me
My culinary creations are courtesy of Peek Freans
Wall's pork pies, Birds Eye peas, Cordon Bleu baked beans

My mum said that children would be the blessing of my life
Would make a loving mother out of a loving wife
I pictured myself baking biscuits and teaching each child how to read
But now I see what I've become, I wonder why I chose to breed – 'cos I've got

Morning sickness, stretch marks on my bum
Varicose veins, I am the 'ideal mum'
They call me Human Dustbin 'cos I won't throw nothing away
So the scraps and the crumbs go down me every day – and I've got

Dishpan hands, housemaid's knee
Hoover elbow, that's what marriage means to me
My culinary creations are courtesy of Peek Freans
Walls pork pies, Birds Eye peas, Cordon Bleu baked beans

My Kids

by Harriet Powell

might dis-cov-er the rea - son ___ if I could stay a-wake, so I'll try. *(yawn)*

⊕ *CODA*

think I'm going to have to go.   ('Tis a bit rude, I know) But all I want to do is go to sleep!

Oh well, it's half past eleven and the kids are in bed
I've watched 'Cagney and Lacey' and I've done the washing-up
And now I'd like to tell you all about the joys of motherhood
But all I want to do is go to sleep

    My kids – argue with each other
    My kids – who would be a mother?
    My kids – I won't be having another
    I think that just the three of them will do

Well there's 'Blue Peter' models made of bog rolls and plastic bottles
Rooms full of drawings they've done since they were two
Playing cards and watching telly, fridge full of rabbit jelly
I really love it all — but why?
Well, I might discover the reason if I could stay awake, so I'll try (YAWN)

Bathroom conversations about all their relations
Counting up the cousins and who belongs to who
'What was it Auntie Rita did to Uncle Peter?'
You've got a lot of explaining to do!
Well, I never let it faze me – some of those things amaze me, too!

Well, I'll be up at half past seven and I'll get them off to school
There'll be a bit of a panic 'I can't find my shoes!' –
Well, I would like to tell you all about the joys of motherhood
But all I want to do is go to sleep (YAWN)

    My kids – run in circles round me
    My kids – bring odd things they've found me
    My kids – stagger and astound me
    Not everyone's cup of tea but they're mine

Breakfast with the teddies, eating lots of shreddies
'Why is it a teddy doesn't go to the loo?'
Stories at bedtime — that's just the best time
Even though they always want 'Winnie the Pooh'.
Well, I don't mind repeating it, I like 'Winnie the Pooh' too!

    My kids – up early in the morning
    My kids – as the day is dawning
    My kids – I'm sorry I keep yawning
    I think I'm going to have to go
    ('Tis a bit rude, I know)
    But all I want to do is go to sleep!

The Tea Party

by Clair Chapman

The following is a lefty's fantasy: tea with two very blue ladies, M . . . T . . . . . . and V . . . . . .
G . . . . Read on, gentle readers.

Gillick: Mrs Thatcher, Mrs Thatcher!
Thatcher: Mrs Gillick, Mrs Gillick!
                    I'm terribly delighted you've invited me for tea
                    The countryside is charming, and the view here is idyllic
                    And the company enchanting –
Gillick: I agree!

                    Mrs Thatcher, Mrs Thatcher, I am honoured you could come here
                    You must have some home-made bread and jam and let me fill your cup
                    There's a lovely little cake that's made of pineapple and plum here
Clair: I'd like a piece of that one –
Thatcher, Gillick: Oh, shut up!

Thatcher: Mrs Gillick, Mrs Gillick, you have been an inspiration
                    In your ruthless fight to ban the pill for girls under sixteen
                    To stamp out wanton pregnancy and sexual liberation
                    And any other nasties in between

Gillick: Mrs Thatcher, Mrs Thatcher, how I blush that you have said it
                    Your thoughts and views on motherhood have given you renown
                    Your values are Victorian, and YOU should take the credit –
Clair: If you want to know what I think —
Thatcher, Gillick: Oh, pipe down!

Thatcher: My tea is slightly strong –
Gillick: Oh dear! I'll have to add some water –
Thatcher: Oh, I almost had forgotten what it was I had to say
                    I think my son is feeling rather keen upon your daughter
                    Have you seen him round about at all this way?

Gillick: There was a chap here last week in a hideous pink Ferrari
                    He skidded through the poultry yard and caused a frightful riot
                    He said his brakes were dodgy, that they'd suffered on safari –
Clair: That's Mark all right!
Thatcher, Gillick: Oh won't you just be quiet!

Gillick: I'm afraid your son's a cad –
Thatcher: I beg your pardon!
Gillick: Frightfully sorry!
                    But Katy's rather young, you see, and he is over-keen
                    A man will stop at nothing to pursue his helpless quarry
                    And after all, she's only just fifteen

Thatcher: It's a bit of fun! A boy and girl – don't get into a lather!
                    Mark has flirtations monthly, Katherine has a schoolgirl crush
                    Remember how you felt when you were her age, if you'd rather –
Clair: Would you like to be a granny?
Thatcher, Gillick: Will you shush!

Gillick:	Can you imagine, Mrs Thatcher, the delight of all the media
	Were your son to get my girl in bed and have his evil way?
	Lefty doctors, Channel Four, I don't know who would be the speedier
	To announce the fact my girl had gone astray
Thatcher:	You are speaking of my son as if he were a common fellow
	Your girl's a piece of skirt that he's just happened to waylay
	Mark's a Gentleman!
Gillick:	I don't think that there's any need to bellow!
Clair:	Oh, I do!
Thatcher, Gillick:	Why don't you just go away!
Gillick:	I'll make just one thing clear: that if my daughter does get preggers
	By your son, who you call Gentleman but I would call a Brute
	It's you and Mr Thatcher who are going to be the beggars
	When I send you the paternity suit!
Thatcher:	Don't threaten me! Your girl's a Tart – it's clear that you've not taught her
	Any guidance about decency has clearly gone amiss
Gillick:	Wretched Baggage! Don't you dare to speak like that about my daughter!
Clair:	If I could have a word –
Thatcher, Gillick:	KEEP OUT OF THIS!
Clair:	Mrs Thatcher, Mrs Thatcher! Mrs Gillick, Mrs Gillick!
	I'm terribly delighted you've invited me for tea
	Your manners are appalling and the tablecloth's acrylic
	And now we'll have a word or two from me
	If your son is not a rapist yet, the Mirror will arrange it
	If your daughter did get pregnant, you would be the last to know
	You've made mileage out of motherhood and, though it may seem
	strange, it
	May well be your downfall. Cheerio!

Three-Hour Mama

by Katina Noble

when I choose. _____ Yes, I'm a

three - hour ___ ma - ma, ___ And I ain't sing - ing those Sex? I'm so knack-er'd! Oh

God! where's your tee-shirt? There's nev - er a mom-ent, Don't pee in that Well - ing - ton

blues. Dar-ling I love you, But

please let me sleep, Be-cause four's a bit ear-ly. Oh, please not the train set! Oh God! not the trum-pet! Oh

Christ! not the ham-ster! Just go back to bed, Will you go back to bed, Oh I see, you've wet it... No,

freely

I ain't sing-ing those twen-ty four __ hour ma-ma __ blues. _____ No way!

They say I ain't natural
I'm weird and I'm a freak
I'll die alone in a council flat
My future's cold and bleak

A woman of my age should have a child
It's the natural thing to do
Well, it's natural for lemmings to jump off that cliff
But what I'm saying to you –

Is it natural to have your eyes forced open at five?
Is it natural not to live but just survive?
Is it natural to stay in ironing every night?
I don't want the whole cherry cheesecake –
all I want is a bite

'Cos I'm a three-hour mama
I do it when I choose
I'm a three-hour mama
And I ain't singing those –
Sex? I'm so knackered!
Oh God! where's your tee-shirt?
There's never a moment
Don't pee in that Wellington – blues

They say I ain't normal
I must have peculiar genes
I never had dollies when I was a girl
Or dresses in my teens

A normal woman's a mother
For twenty four hours a day
Well I like 'em, I love 'em, I leave 'em
Hand them back and walk away

Is it normal to be treated like a slave?
Is is normal to never go out and rave?
Is it normal to always pretend you're strong?
If I didn't have some time to myself I couldn't have written this song

'Cos I'm a three-hour mama
I do it when I choose
I'm a three-hour mama
And I ain't singing those –
      Please put your toys away
      Don't pull the budgie's tail
      Sit on that potty, now
      Don't eat the Kit-e-Kat – blues

Yes, I'm a three-hour mama
I do it when I choose
I'm a three-hour mama
And I ain't singing those –
      Darling, I love you
      But please let me sleep
      Because four's a bit early
      Oh please not the train set!
      Oh God! not the trumpet!
      Oh Christ! not the hamster!
      Just go back to bed
      Will you go back to bed –
      Oh, I see – you've wet it...

No, I ain't singing those twenty-four hour mama blues –
      NO WAY!

Angst Unlimited

We have discovered a wonderful way of dealing with emotional pain. We talk about it in the van and then we turn it into a song or sketch.

'He's left me'

'I'm tired of being on my own'

'Is non-monogamy really a viable concept in a bourgeois society?'

'Write it down'

'Get out your notebook, kid'

'I'll loan you my tape recorder for the weekend'

These are some of the results.

How Do You Talk To A Boy?

by Clair Chapman

How do you talk to a boy? How do you know how to start off?

How do you talk to a boy? _____ Please tell me how to be - gin. _____ I've

spent the whole day in a bath of Cam-ay, Learn-ing the scores on the bask-et-ball charts. I've

hoped that the flash-es of well paint-ed lash-es would lead to the meet-ing of two beat-ing hearts. I've

curl-ed my hair, put per-fume ev-'ry-where And paint-ed my nails with 'Vi-o-let Vix-en', Read

'Time' mag-a-zine so I'm up on the scene, Jack-ie O-nas-sis, Pres-i-dent Nix-on.

He'd leave me, the cad! I'd dis-grace Mom and Dad, I'd have to leave school and my

home and my friends In the deep-en-ing gloom of a dark lit-tle room. I'd kill my-self! This is the end!

How do you talk to a boy?
How do you know how to start off?
How do you talk to a boy?
Please tell me how to begin

I've spent the whole day in a bath of Camay
Learning the scores on the basketball charts
I've hoped that the flashes of well painted lashes
Would lead to the meeting of two beating hearts

I've curled my hair, put perfume everywhere
And painted my nails with Violet Vixen
Read Time magazine so I'm up on the scene
Jackie Onassis – President Nixon

   How do you talk to a boy?
   Don't think we speak the same language
   How do you talk to a boy?
   I just don't know what to say

He's covered in warts and he doesn't like sports
And his nose is all pimply and he looks like a
                        horse
And his teeth are all grey (doesn't brush every
                        day)
Shall I ask if his parents are getting divorced?

His breath is all hot and he's blowing out snot
All over my shoulder (he's not very tall!)
His nails caked with dirt, there's a hole in his
                        shirt

And I don't think he cares about Nixon at all

What would I do with a boy
Once I had finally caught him?
What would I do with a boy
Once I was wearing his ring?

We'd sit on the couch and he'd slump in a slouch
And I'd sit very straight like a queen in a play
And I would look down and he'd look around
And we'd struggle for anything – something to
                        say

And then when he found there was no one
                        around
He'd put his arm round me and fondle my breast
And then he'd do more and we'd be on the floor
And I don't have to tell you, you know all the rest –

He'd leave me – the cad! I'd disgrace Mom and
                        Dad
I'd have to leave school and my home and my
                        friends
In the deepening gloom of a dark little room
I'd kill myself! This is the end!

   Why am I wanting a boy?
   Only can lead into trouble
   Why am I wanting a boy?
   Think I'll have something to eat

Saturday Night

by Clair Chapman

Tonight I can't deny
I am way down and I just want to cry
I could cheer me up but I don't care to try
'Cos I got the blues bad, let me tell you why . . .

It's Saturday night and I'm watching the big fight on TV
I've pulled all the curtains so I can be certain
That none of the neighbours will see me
And there's nothing to watch on a Saturday night
'Cos you're s'posed to be raving it up tonight, right?
On Saturday night when I'm watching the big fight on TV

It's Saturday night and the underwear's white on the TV
Snowy fresh on the line – I ought to do mine
Oh, hell, no one sees it except me
I s'pose that I might just get hit by a bus
But not in my sitting room, so what's the fuss?
On Saturday night when the underwear's white on the TV

Can't stand the sight
Folks going out in twos, coming back tight
I think I'll go to bed and put out the light
'Cos nothing is worse than this Saturday night . . .

It's Saturday night and the whole world is all right except me
They're screwing like crazy, tomorrow they'll be lazy
And I will be doing my laundry
Will this go on, week after week 'til I'm buried?
I see now why so many people get married
On Saturday night when the whole world is all right
(I know it's not true) oh, but why does it seem like
On Saturday night that the whole world is all right – except me?

Oh well it looks like chicken and chips for one in the launderette again

SNOOZZE

actually some people find my company quite stimulating

Macaroons

by Clair Chapman

Dramatically

I was going to write a song a-bout how great it is to be a-lone, Thing is that I could-n't, 'cos it is - n't. I was going to write a song a-bout how great it is being in - de-pen-dent But I real-ly could-n't, 'cos it stinks. As I sit here, moans and screams of pas-sion drift down from a-bove, They groan and shriek to-geth - er, he says 'darl - ing', she says 'love'. Then they'll curl up and he'll hold her and he'll warm her back in spoons. I've got my lit-tle green hot-wat-er bot-tle and a bag of mac-a-roons! gon-na fuck-in' scream! (screams) Who'll hold my hand when we go to the mov-ies? Who'll hold my hand when we go on hol-i-day? Who'll hold my hand when they fin-al-ly drop Po-lar-is? I guess it does-n't mat-ter, an-y - way.

64

Oh, I was going to write a song a-bout how great it is to be a-lone.

Well, some-times I guess... it could be worse!

I was going to write a song about how great it is to be alone
Thing is that I couldn't, 'cos it isn't

I was going to write a song about how great it is being independent
But I really couldn't, 'cos it stinks

As I sit here, moans and screams of passion drift down from above
They groan and shriek together, he says 'darling' she says 'love'
Then they'll curl up and he'll hold her and he'll warm her back in spoons
I've got my little green hot-water bottle and a bag of macaroons!

I was going to write a song about how great it is to be alone
But I really couldn't, 'cos it ain't

If I hear her say any more how much in love she is
And how he looks into her green-flecked eyes and she looks into his
How they are always holding hands, how they shared an ice cream
How they make love twelve times a day I'm gonna fuckin' scream! (SCREAM)

    Who'll hold my hand when we go to the movies?
    Who'll hold my hand when we go on holiday?
    Who'll hold my hand when they finally drop Polaris?
    I guess it doesn't matter, anyway

I was going to write a song about how great it is to be alone
If I did I think I might throw up

What's that? The sound of breaking glass? 'You bitch!' 'You sod!' 'You cow!'
Sound of screaming, sound of yelling and deadly silence now
And then, the sound of weeping as I turn out my light,
'I thought you said you loved me!' as I pull my covers tight

Oh, I was going to write a song about how great it is to be alone
Well – sometimes I guess . . . it could be worse!

from now on it'll be just you 'n' me kid!

Guilt

by Clair Chapman

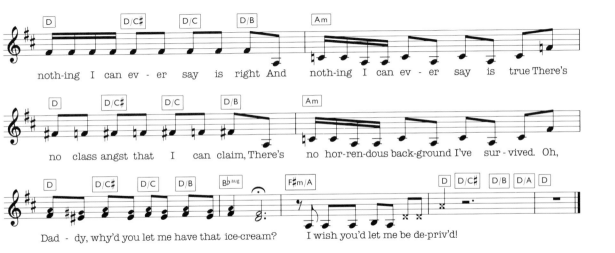

nothing I can ever say is right And nothing I can ever say is true There's no class angst that I can claim, There's no horrendous background I've survived. Oh, Daddy, why'd you let me have that ice-cream? I wish you'd let me be depriv'd!

(Guilt! Guilt! Guilt! Guilt! Guilt! Guilt! Guilt! Guilt!)

    Guilty. I feel guilty. I feel guilty every time I realize
    That I grew up with an inside loo and he grew up in a slum
    Guilt, I feel guilt. I feel
    Guilty. I feel guilty. I feel guilty about the privilege I've had
    What a piece of cake it's all been for me, what he's had to overcome
    I feel guilt

Growing up for me was super seaside holidays, what fun!
'Daddy, can I have an ice-cream?' 'Yes, my sweet, I'll buy you one'
Growing up for him was drunken fights and screaming rows instead
'Father, Father, don't hit Mother!' 'Shut up kid, I'll break your head!'

(Guilt! Guilt! Guilt! Guilt!)

    Guilty. I feel guilty. I feel guilty every time I remember I'm
    A member of a class that deserves to be stood up and each one shot
    I feel guilt

Still I wish (sometimes!) that I could also claim his class credential
When he speaks at meetings he is always very influential
Speeches that I make (that are as sound) can often go unheard
'She is only middle-class and just a silly bird!'

(Guilt! Guilt! Guilt! Guilt!)

    Guilty. I feel guilty. I feel guilty every time I realize
    (And possible a little angry, too)
    That nothing I can ever say is right
    And nothing I can ever say is true
    There's no class angst that I can claim
    There's no horrendous background I've survived
    Oh, Daddy, why'd you let me have that ice cream?
    I wish you'd let me – be deprived!

Banana Splits

by Clair Chapman

Bossa nova

Did you ev-er stop to think there's two diff-'rent class-es? No, not Hack-ney and the

Ritz, I'm talk-ing a-bout those whose life is ce-ler-y And those whose life is ban-a-na splits.

CHORUS

Well, it's just like that, You've got to ac-cept it. ___

Yes, it's just like that, ___ It's real-ly the pits.

Yes, that's your lot, girl, And you can look for-ward

last time
D.$ al Coda

to Coda

To a life-time of cel-er-y ___ No ban-a-na splits.

CODA

No ban-a-na splits, No ban-a-na

splits, No ban-a-na splits, ban-a-na splits!

Did you ever stop to think there's two different classes?
No, not Hackney and the Ritz –
I'm talking about those whose life is celery
And those whose life is banana splits

Everywhere she looks there's Farrah and Brooke Shields
Aerobics make her want to cry
While her old man's fine at any size
Pigging out on apple pie

    CHORUS
    Well it's just like that
    You've got to accept it
    Yes it's just like that
    It's really the pits
    Yes, that's your lot, girl
    And you can look forward
    To a lifetime of celery
    No banana splits

You get used to watching him change a plug
Thinking you could never learn
You get used to opening his wages
Seeing double what you earn

You get used to 'Get 'em off there, darling'
'Drop 'em, sexy chick!'
You get used to playing the mating game
Dancing around the sacred dick

    CHORUS and then:
    No banana splits
    No banana splits, banana splits!

Men Are Like That

by Clair Chapman

This one is sung to the tune of 'Banana Splits', beginning with the chorus

CHORUS
Men are just like that
You've got to expect it
Yes, men are like that
They're just little boys
Yes, men are like that
They're big babies really
Their cars are important
Their women are toys

1st Secretary
Let me tell you about my husband Mike
He likes a nice cup of tea
So I give him one and sit down for a chat
And he turns on the TV!

Or we've polished off a litre of Pomagne
It's been a month, I've really got the hots
So I swan in in my see-through negligée
He says, 'Can't you do something about your spots?'

CHORUS

2nd Secretary
Let me tell you about my new boyfriend Don
He says that he will come round at the weekend
So I cook fillet steaks in cream
He rings up — he's gone fishing in Southend

The flat's a mess, dirty clothes everywhere
In the kitchen not even one clean cup
Watching 'Dallas' my vibrator in my hand
And three guesses who turns up!

CHORUS

1st Secretary
You get used to being at his beck and call
You get used to always cleaning out the loo
You get used to never getting your own way
And being told you always do

2nd Secretary
You get used to waiting for the pub to close
You get used to always being let down
You get used to saying no to friends in case
Your superman comes round

CHORUS

I Think I'm Gonna Be Sick

by Katina Noble

Mine is an open relationship – non-monogamous and free.
How can we struggle with sexual politics enslaved by jealousy?

I've never really liked couples, so smug in their unwedded bliss.
Stifled by insecurities: 'Bill and I think this ... and this.'

We've no right to possess anyone, saying 'Sorry, he's mine'
Of course you can love more than one person! It's natural! It's fine!

He stayed out last night – no problem! But is seeing her again today ...
You mean this is ongoing? Not just lust in the dark? I smile in a feeble way

You're strong enough to cope with this. Maybe they won't click?
He says she won't want to get involved – but I think I'm gonna be sick.

Friday night. They're in her bed now. I wonder if she's got a duvet?
Wonder if her thighs are thinner than mine? Wonder how long he'll stay?

Now, come on! You know this is no threat. He's your lover and your friend
This is politically very right on – but when is it going to end?

Will they linger in bed all morning – a smile, a touch, a lick?
Gaze at each other over boiled eggs and toast? I think I'm gonna be sick.

Well, I try reading 'The Politics of Sex in the Bourgeois Family in Patriarchal
Structures Under Capitalism', but that is no help at all

I try meditation ... T'ai Chi . . . Valium . . . but all I do is bawl
Weep, whimper, sob, gulp back the tears
Do you need a prescription for cyanide? This could go on for years!

But I won't fall into the old scenario – 'He's a bastard. She's a bitch' –
That game's built on dishonesty, but there's just one tiny hitch –

My body cannot cope with this. Guts churning, head heavy and thick
Maybe there's something in celibacy – I think I'm gonna be sick.

Well I haven't got all the answers, but I won't give in to this.
I'd rather face feelings than sink into unthinking, monogamous bliss.

It's light now. He's not back yet. God, I hope it's over quick.
Anyone got a bucket? I KNOW I'm gonna be sick!

Gonna Be Some Changes

by Clair Chapman

Gonna be some changes made around here
You can call me darling or dear as much as you like
But it's on your bike
If you don't make changes around here

Won't eat my heart out anymore
I won't scrub your kitchen floor
Or bake your bread or make your bed
Won't eat my heart out anymore

Ooh baby, gonna turn your head around
Changes gonna happen every day
Ooh baby, gonna knock you to the ground
You might even wish you stayed away!

Ain't gonna watch you watch TV
Sit for hours and not talk to me
Or fix your grub while you're down the pub
Ain't gonna watch you watch TV

Ooh baby, you thought that it would take
A cuddle and a kiss to open my door
Ooh, you thought it was gonna be a piece of cake
Well, you had just better think some more!

Gonna be some changes made around here
Gonna be a brand new atmosphere
And we're gonna be friends or that's the end
Gonna be some changes made around here

Laugh Lines

It says here that if you give up meat, sugar, fat, coffee, alcohol, smoking, sex and emotionally demanding situations you could live to be 100.

Since when was that living?

A show about ageing? No, we're not ready for that. Jesus, I've got another grey hair. We'll do 'Laugh Lines' when we're forty-seven. You know, OLD. What is that under my eye? An eyelash? Or another wrinkle? Christ, I've never put Erase there before.... Ooh. Shall we go to that party in Brixton? It's too far. Not worth the hangover, shall we go to the pub? Let's make a cup of tea and watch 'Dallas'.

A Million Billion Lemmings Can't Be Wrong

by Clair Chapman

Country & western

I grew up in Minnesota where the winters were cold and long, One freezing, snowy day I thought I'd put some long pants on, At last! I could walk to school without my kneecaps starting to hurt, But my teacher stood at the classroom door, said 'You gotta wear a skirt.'

'Cause a hundred little schoolgirls can't be wrong, can they, A hundred little schoolgirls can't be wrong Only boys wear pants, you look a mess, You're not coming in 'til you're wearing a dress, A hundred little schoolgirls can't be wrong

I saluted the flag each morning, I grew up brave and strong,
Learned about freedom, brushing my teeth, learned that the bad guys were wrong,
In 1968 the US went to Vietnam
I didn't know who the bad guys were and so I asked my mom.

   She said, a hundred million Americans can't be wrong, honey,
   A hundred million Americans can't be wrong,
   You might think the other guys are right,
   It's very confusing, don't worry, sleep tight,
   'Cause a hundred million Americans can't be wrong.

I had boyfriend after boyfriend through many many years,
I remember one painful argument watered with my tears,
I said, 'I've given everything I've got:
Warmth-affection-support-sex-security and positive reinforcement to name but a few,
There's not a whole lot coming back, what do I get from you?

   He said, 'A billion heterosexuals can't be wrong, baby,
   A billion heterosexuals can't be wrong,
   I'll provide the sex 'til the end,
   Get the other stuff from a friend,
   'Cause a billion heterosexuals can't be wrong.'

Then I died and went to heaven and I came back as a lemming,
The first day the lemming next door asked me out to go swimming,
I said that I was scared, she said, 'You fool! don't make a fuss,
Just throw yourself right over the cliff like the rest of us.'

   'Cause a million billion lemmings can't be wrong, can they,
   A million billion lemmings can't be wrong,
   Just start to run and close your eyes tight,
   We've done it for centuries, it must be right,
   A million billion lemmings can't be wrong!

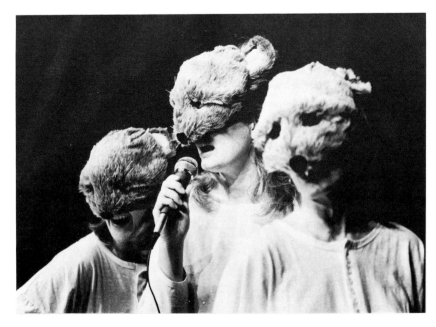

The Alternative (Seventies) Boogie-woogie

by Harriet Powell

where it's all at __ so why am I just sit-ting here at home feel-ing fat? It's

D. C. al 𝄋

true that equ-al-it-y is here for some so why am I still wait-ing for my prince to come?

Collectivism – Feminism – Socialism – Idealism –
Demonstrations, Occupations, Revolution, Revelation!

CHORUS
This is it! The seventies boogie woogie,
That's right! It's revolutionary,
Right-on! You better believe it,
Fight on! We're gonna achieve it,
The seventies boogie woogie, let's live!
It's the only boogie woogie that's alternative!

We're the people that our parents warned us about,
Join the revolution, let it all hang out,
Lentil stew for thirty-two and dungarees,
This is what will bring the country to its knees,
Power to the people, we're gonna unite,
Our parents are wrong and we are right!

CHORUS

It's true the revolution is for me and you,
So why are they all out there and I'm stirring the stew,
It's true that liberation is where it's all at,
So why am I just sitting here at home feeling fat?
It's true that equality is here for some,
So why am I still waiting for my prince to come?

CHORUS

Our liberated language makes our parents freak,
They never understand a single word that we speak,
Do your own thing, Alexander Technique,
Right-on, Rev Speak, it's unique,
The capitalist system will go down the drain,
And nothing's ever gonna be the same again!

CHORUS

It's A Phase

by Harriet Powell

CHORUS
It's a phase (like the moon), just a craze,
There'll be a new phase soon,
She'll grow out of it,
There's no doubt of it,
It's a phase (oh, the ways these days!)
They like to torture you,
It can't go on forever,
No they never do!

She's been a wonderful daughter,
We've never really fought her,
Over anything she wanted to do.
Now it may be just a fad,
But this one's awfully bad,
She isn't eating meat, she's a vegetarian!
(Oh, the shame of it)

CHORUS

Now she is, oh, so charming,
And this is quite alarming,
To see her breaking the rules.
Well, I hope it's over soon,
She's, well, in a commune,
With lots of other people, cats and children
(Oh, the pain of it)

CHORUS

She's been such a good girl,
They even made her head girl,
At school, she had her feet on the ground.
Now, oh, how do I begin?
Well, she's living in sin,
Having children. She's an unmarried mum!
(Oh, my God)

CHORUS
It's a phase (like the moon), just a craze,
There'll be a new phase soon,
She'll grow out of it,
There's no doubt of it,
It's a phase (oh, the ways these days!)
They try to amaze you,
Well, it can't go on for long,
No, they'll see we're right, they're wrong.
In a very short while, they'll be totally out of style.

They'll have to conform and behave like the norm,
These phases will go as we mothers all know,
At the end of the day, we will try not to say...

We told you so!

encore

Woke Up This Morning
by Clair Chapman

Rhythm & blues - bags of raunch (and paunch)

(spoken introductions:)

Woke up this morn-ing ___ and I put on ___ two pounds, ___ Woke up this morn-ing ___ and I put on ___ two pounds, You bet-ter hand me two tape meas-ures 'Cos one ain't gon-na go a-round. ___ and I said: Ain't you jeal-ous, cheek-y chum? Skin-ny lit-tle thighs and ti-ny bum, Bet you've weigh'd the same since age six-teen. Ti-ny chest and your ribs show through, A skel-e-ton's chub-by next ___ to you, You'd lose a con-test with the string-i-est bean.

Ladies and gentlemen, for your delight tonight, all the way from sunny South Camden, triumphant mother of two and colossus of two keyboards and my very good friend. Ladies and gentlemen will you put your hands together for –

Harriet!

And on drums, for the very first time, her very good friend, city girl, socialist, and the compulsive eating queen –

Teen!

And on vocals, all the way from the US of A, currently hanging out everywhere, but at this moment right here, ladies and gentlemen, I give you myself:

Clair!

Woke up this morning and I put on two pounds (Oh, no, baby, no!)
Woke up this morning and I put on two pounds (Oh, no, baby, no!)
You better hand me two tape measures
'Cos one ain't gonna go around

Woke up this morning and my jeans didn't fit (Oh, shame baby, shame!)
Woke up this morning and my jeans didn't fit (Shame, shame, shame!)
And all the safety pins in England
Ain't gonna help it one little bit

Got outta bed and I could feel my bottom shake (Let that ass shake!)
Got outta bed and I could feel my bottom shake (Let that big ass shake!)
Someday I'm gonna jump out
And the whole world's gonna break (right in two, oh yeah!)

Got outta bed and I could feel my jelly belly (Let that jelly roll!)
Got outta bed and I could feel my jelly belly (Let that jelly roll!)
Look like a fat-assed lady
Painted by Mr Botticelli

Walked down the road and I heard a fella snigger (Hah!)
Walked down the road and I heard a fella snigger (Hah!)
He was a-laughin at my body
Inside of me it pulled the trigger – and I said:

Ain't you jealous, cheeky chum?
Skinny little thighs and tiny bum
Bet you've weighed the same since age sixteen

Tiny chest and your ribs show through
A skeleton's chubby next to you
You'd lose a contest with the stringiest bean

I bet when they bury you
You will still be nine stone two
Hope it makes you happy, baby
Spiky hips don't do it for me – uh uh

I like me just the way I am
So shove off baby, beat it, scram!
Hit the road, Jack — piss off, flake!
And find yourself a baby – try the garden rake
                                              – 'cos I got

Breasts and hips and bum and thighs
Man – you better believe your eyes
A pretty big girl as you can see –
No one messes around with me!

When I'm walking, night or day
Let some man dare go 'WAY — HEY!'
They better not do that to this girl
'Cos I'm a great big mama – and I run my world!